"Lent requires preparation, and this book shows us how to do just that. Esau McCaulley's *Lent* is an invitation to live into the Scriptures, practices, and prayers of Lent afresh, calling and equipping us to experience the gravity of sin, but also the expanse of God's grace and mercy. Whether you are a new or seasoned observer of Lent, this book is invaluable preparation to live into the contrition and true repentance to which this holy season invites us."

Teesha Hadra, rector of Church of the Resurrection Los Angeles and author of *Black and White: Disrupting Racism One Friendship at a Time*

"Esau McCaulley has given Christ-followers a gift. But like all gifts, you have to receive it and open it up. In *Lent: The Season of Repentance and Renewal*, Esau updates the ancient pathway of Lent so we can connect deeper with Jesus, his church, and his kingdom."

Derwin L. Gray, author of *How to Heal Our Racial Divide*

"Esau McCaulley is a gift. He is the rare blend of a first-rate mind married to a huge heart for God and neighbor. This neighborliness comes out in two ways. As a public theologian writing for the *New York Times* and others, Esau shows his ability to provide clear thinking at the intersection of church and culture. In *Lent: The Season of Repentance and Renewal*, Esau shows his pastor's heart, his love for the church, and his passion to help Christians grow in faith. I commend *Lent* to everyone who is curious about, or committed to, the practice of Lent in their local church."

Todd Hunter, Anglican bishop and author of *Deep Peace: Finding Calm in a World of Conflict and Anxiety*

"Esau McCaulley says in this book that 'God's grace meets us again and again.' It's a timely message for the church and the reader. May we be renewed as we repent, and may God meet us on this journey again and again."

Heather Thompson Day, author of *It's Not Your Turn*

Esau McCaulley

Esau McCaulley, SERIES EDITOR

Lent

The Season of Repentance and Renewal

Fullness of Time series

An imprint of InterVarsity Press

Downers Grove, Illinois

InterVarsity Press
P.O. Box 1400 | Downers Grove, IL 60515-1426
ivpress.com | email@ivpress.com

InterVarsity Press® is the publishing division of InterVarsity Christian Fellowship/USA®. For more information, visit intervarsity.org.

All Scripture quotations, unless otherwise indicated, are taken from The Holy Bible, New International Version®, NIV®. Copyright © 1973, 1978, 1984, 2011 by Biblica, Inc.™ Used by permission of Zondervan. All rights reserved worldwide. www.zondervan.com. The "NIV" and "New International Version" are trademarks registered in the United States Patent and Trademark Office by Biblica, Inc.™

While any stories in this book are true, some names and identifying information may have been changed to protect the privacy of individuals.

The publisher cannot verify the accuracy or functionality of website URLs used in this book beyond the date of publication.

Cover design and image composite: David Fassett
Interior design: Daniel van Loon

ISBN 978-1-5140-0048-9 (print) | ISBN 978-1-5140-0049-6 (digital)

Printed in the United States of America ♾

Library of Congress Cataloging-in-Publication Data
Names: McCaulley, Esau, author.
Title: Lent : the season of repentance and renewal / Esau McCaulley.
Description: Downers Grove, IL : InterVarsity Press, [2022] | Series: Fullness of time ; book 1 | Includes bibliographical references.
Identifiers: LCCN 2022024554 (print) | LCCN 2022024555 (ebook) | ISBN 9781514000489 (print) | ISBN 9781514000496 (digital)
Subjects: LCSH: Lent.
Classification: LCC BV85 .M155 2022 (print) | LCC BV85 (ebook) | DDC 242/.34--dc23/eng/20220701
LC record available at https://lccn.loc.gov/2022024554
LC ebook record available at https://lccn.loc.gov/2022024555

28 27 26 25 24 23 22 | 11 10 9 8 7 6 5 4 3 2 1

This book is dedicated to my wife, Mandy.

*It is my great joy to journey through the church year
and life with you as we pursue Christ together.*

Contents

The Fullness of Time

SERIES PREFACE

ESAU MCCAULLEY, GENERAL EDITOR

Christians of all traditions are finding a renewed appreciation for the church year. This is evident in the increased number of churches that mark the seasons in their preaching and teaching. It's evident in the families and small groups looking for ways to recover ancient practices of the Christian faith. This is all very good. To assist in this renewal, we thought Christians might find it beneficial to have an accessible guide to the church year, one that's more than a devotional but less than an academic tome.

The Fullness of Time project aims to do just that. We have put together a series of short books on the seasons and key events of the church year, including Advent,

Christmas, Epiphany, Lent, Easter, and Pentecost. These books are reflections on the moods, themes, rituals, prayers, and Scriptures that mark each season.

These are not, strictly speaking, devotionals. They are theological and spiritual reflections that seek to provide spiritual formation by helping the reader live fully into the practices of each season. We want readers to understand how the church is forming them in the likeness of Christ through the church calendar.

These books are written from the perspective of those who have lived through the seasons many times, and we'll use personal stories and experiences to explain different aspects of the season that are meaningful to us. In what follows, do not look for comments from historians pointing out minutiae. Instead, look for fellow believers and evangelists using the tool of the church year to preach the gospel and point Christians toward discipleship and spiritual formation. We pray that these books will be useful to individuals, families, and churches seeking a deeper walk with Jesus.

We Must Repent

An Introduction to Lent

"The time has come," he said. "The kingdom of God has come near. Repent and believe the good news!"

Mark 1:15

Lent is inescapably about repenting. Repentance is a change in direction, a Spirit-empowered turning around. Repentance, then, is the first step we make toward God. But to turn toward God we must turn away from something else. That something else is our sins.

Lent, then, is about turning away from our sins and toward the living God. A season dedicated to repentance and renewal should not lead us to despair; it should cause us to praise God for his grace. Central to Lent is the idea that we need this kind of renewal consistently throughout our lives. We do not receive God's grace only when we turn to him at the beginning of our spiritual journey. God's grace meets us again and again.

Repentance solves the crisis created by our initial encounter with the gospel and its central character: the Messiah Jesus. Therefore, we cannot begin to discuss what Lent is until we do a little more to outline the shape of repentance.

When Peter preached that first sermon at Pentecost, the Scripture says his hearers were "cut to the heart" and asked, "What shall we do?" (Acts 2:37). Peter told them they must repent. The proclamation of the gospel and the realization that it tells the story of God's work through his Son's life, death, and resurrection creates a crisis. When we enter the presence of God, no one has to convince us of our sinfulness. We learn about our inadequacy by the contrast between ourselves and God's holiness.

When I encountered Jesus, I knew I was in the presence not merely of a better person but of a different category of being altogether, the God-Man. We see the inadequacy of our former way of life in the light of the holiness of God's Son.

This is why this same apostle, when he first glimpsed Jesus during the miraculous catch of fish, said, "Go away from me, Lord; I am a sinful man!" (Luke 5:8). It's why Isaiah, when he encountered the presence of God, could only cry, "Woe to me!" (Isaiah 6:5).

The good news is that at the moment we see the gap between ourselves and our Lord, we also encounter the blood that draws us in and assures us we are forgiven. Jesus' own presence is both grace and judgment.

I don't remember much about what led me to be baptized at an early age, but I do remember the feeling of dread that came over me then, and many other times over the years. It's a dread that has come over all those who come to Jesus. It's the thrill and the terror that the story of Jesus—his life, death, resurrection, ascension, and eventual return—is true. If these things are true, everything is turned upside down. The life we have known is ended; something new has begun. God help us, we must change direction. We must repent.

While repentance is required of new followers of Jesus making their first steps toward God, it is also the means by which all followers of Jesus start again when we have failed. Luther begins his famous Ninety-Five Theses by saying, "When our Lord and Master Jesus Christ said, 'Repent' (Matthew 4:17), he willed the entire life of believers to be one of repentance."[1] The goal of beginning again and beginning for the first time is the same. We are seeking communion with the risen Lord.

Lent is a season of repentance and preparation. In many churches, it is a time when those who will be baptized prepare for their new life with God. It is a time when those who have been estranged from the church can be reconciled to the body of believers. It is also a time for all of us to think about the ways we have drifted from the faith. The common theme uniting these three functions of Lent is that they all involve a turning toward God with intention and reflection on the past.

We hope that as Christians we mature and grow and become more and more like Christ. But the church in its wisdom assumes we will fail, even after our baptism. The church presumes that life is long and zeal fades, not just for some of us but for all. So it has included within its life a season in which all of us can recapture our love for God and his kingdom and cast off those things that so easily entangle us.

Today Lent is observed as forty days of fasting in preparation for Easter. In the West, Lent begins on Ash Wednesday and concludes on Holy Saturday, the day before Easter. Exactly how we ended up with this period of time is something of a mystery. In the first few centuries of the church's life, believers observed a one- or two-day fast in preparation for Easter. Some scholars think this fast was eventually extended to what we now call Holy Week. We went from a few days to a week of preparation. One week grew to three weeks and eventually to forty days. During those forty days, baptismal candidates were prepared to be received into the church on Easter.[2]

As best we can tell, however, the fasts related to Holy Week developed apart from what is now called Lent. It seems there was a period of fasting that preceded baptism even when the baptism was not connected with Easter.[3] Those fasts varied in length, but there is some evidence that the forty-day pre-baptismal fast was popular in Alexandria.

However Lent precisely developed, it's clear the early Christians thought baptism was serious and required preparation. I think this is wise. Becoming a Christian is no small matter. To transition from believing you live in a world where death is the end, to one in which an almighty God calls dead things to life, is much more significant than choosing what to have for breakfast. We should have space to reflect on the full significance of the change.

After the Council of Nicaea set a particular date for the celebration of Easter, many throughout the church began to see the Feast of the Resurrection as the best time to bring people into the church. It was also a fitting time to bring back those who had strayed. The link between Lent and Easter then was a collision of different factors. The season of fasting linked to baptism and the reconciliation of those estranged from the church were connected to the fasting undertaken in preparation for Easter, including Holy Week.

So Lent came to be about three things: the preparation of new converts for baptism, the reconciliation of those estranged from the church, and a general call for the whole church to repent and renew its commitment to Jesus.

In those early centuries, the practice varied. In the East, the Lenten fast lasted seven weeks, but Saturdays and Sundays weren't counted in the total, so there were actually only thirty-six fast days.[4] In the West, the fast was only six weeks, but they too ended up with thirty-six days because Sundays were not counted.[5] Western Christians eventually added the four days from Ash Wednesday to the First Sunday of Lent to give us the number forty.

Today in most Western churches the days of Lent are calculated by counting forty days from Ash Wednesday through the end of Holy Week, excluding Sundays.

Fasting practices also differed. In some contexts particular foods were removed from the diet during Lent; in others the number of meals was reduced. This might seem like the kind of creeping legalism that sends Protestants running for the hills. But hold on.

All this variation is actually freeing. There is no single way to observe Lent given from on high that we must follow to be right with God. The history of Lent is like our spiritual lives. The church stumbled around trying different things in order to discern the best ways to use this time to grow closer to God. We should not see the season of Lent as a series of rules but as a gift of the collected wisdom of the church universal. It is one of many tools of discipleship pointing us toward a closer walk with Jesus.

This does not mean we should treat Lent as a spiritual buffet to pick and choose from arbitrarily. It means we should take the wisdom the church offers as just that— wisdom. There may be some benefit to adopting practices that don't initially make sense to us because Christians before us have struggled, discerned, and prayed their way into the traditions that are now our heritage.

I was not baptized at the end of Lent. I was raised in the Black Baptist church, where we got baptized when we heard the gospel and believed. But Lent does hold a particular place in my heart. The season of Lent was my first encounter with liturgical spirituality. It added a new element to my spiritual life.

My first Lent was a pilgrimage. I did not leave the city I resided in, but I did go on a journey. At a time when I felt adrift spiritually, Lent helped me become aware of the nearness of God. These outward practices took me on an inward journey further into the awareness of God.

That is the purpose of all of this. In this series of books on the liturgical seasons, we aren't trying to lay further burdens on the backs of Christians or pretend we've figured out the only way to please God. Instead, these are notes on an encounter that is available to all.

What follows is an attempt to point out the things I've seen along the way. It is not just an explanation of Lent but an invitation to experience it, a chance to meet our risen Lord who always runs just ahead of us, beckoning us forward.

I

Facing Death, Finding Hope

Ash Wednesday

Remember that you are dust and to dust you shall return.

Recited during the imposition of ashes
on the first day of Lent

All lives end. Black lives and White lives, Asian lives and Latina lives, the young and the old, men and women. Some will die terrified to their last moment. Some will pass away in deep pain and anguish. Others will say their final words surrounded by loved ones who quietly chant the Psalter. Some will die in elder care centers, alone and forgotten. We die in a thousand different ways, glorious and mundane. It's the universal characteristic of the human condition.

Yet we push death and its signals away. We dye our gray hair, trade in glasses for contacts or vision surgery, and add a mile or two to our runs. We do all we can to ignore death's presence or wish it away, including hiding the elderly and infirm from sight in nursing homes and hospitals. But death is coming and we must face it.

Paul refers to death as "the last enemy to be destroyed" (1 Corinthians 15:26). He says that when the Messiah defeats death, his people will say, "Where, O death, is your victory? Where, O death, is your sting?" (1 Corinthians 15:55). But until we have been raised from the dead and death has been swallowed up in victory, it still stings and wounds. I carry the deaths of my father and the two children we lost to miscarriage in my heart. I carry the deaths of Black boys and girls lost to police violence and gang brutality. We carry the deaths of innocents all over the world with us. Let's tell the truth. Death hurts.

What's in a Name? Ash Wednesday

Lent begins with Ash Wednesday, a service known for the imposition of ashes. As clergy mark the foreheads of the faithful, we tell them, "Remember that you are dust, and to dust you shall return." We tell them they are going to die.

I remember serving as a priest on Ash Wednesday after I was married and had small children. Kids get excited about everything in church that's different from the norm, so the idea of coming down the aisle to receive something new thrilled them. Instead of Communion they got their foreheads marked with ashes. I experienced something far from excitement or joy. I looked at my wife and two young children and told them words that broke me. I told them they would return to dust, and as a symbol of that returning, I marked their foreheads with ashes in the shape of the cross.

In the Bible, ashes are a sign of mourning and loss. When Xerxes issued a command to kill all the Jews in his kingdom, the Israelites responded in the following way: "In every province to which the edict and order of the king came, there was great mourning among the Jews, with fasting, weeping and wailing. Many lay in sackcloth and ashes" (Esther 4:3). The link between mourning and ashes is well established in the Scriptures (see Daniel 9:3; Jeremiah 6:26; Job 42:6; Matthew 11:21).

The liturgy makes a second connection as well, one that goes beyond the symbols of repentance found in biblical depictions of mourning. It takes us back to the origin of all our pain. Ash Wednesday evokes the punishment arising from the fall, when God says to Adam and Eve,

"Dust you are and to dust you will return" (Genesis 3:19). In other words, the sadness of Lent is not a general sadness about the inevitability of death but an explicitly Christian diagnosis of the cause of death. We sin and die because humanity rebelled against God. There is nothing natural at all about death. It is an alien intrusion into the good world God created. It is an enemy to be defeated. On Ash Wednesday we remember that we will die, but we do not accept it as the inevitable reality of the human experience. Even in our acknowledgment of death there are hints of our rebellion against it.

We sin and die because we are born in the aftermath of the rebellion of our first parents. Adam and Eve rebelled because they wanted to be like God and were led away by their desires (Genesis 3:5-6). They believed the serpent's lie and disobeyed God's command (Genesis 3:13). This rebellion had implications that spread out in multiple directions, including engendering a new distrust of each other (Genesis 3:7) and of God (Genesis 3:8-9).

Through the imposition of ashes, Ash Wednesday reminds us that death and sin cannot be completely separated. This does not mean a particular form of death is punishment for specific sins, but sin and death are partners.

But if the ashes of Ash Wednesday point us toward the link between sin, death, and rebellion, they also contain something else, something more important than everything we have seen thus far. The ashes are in the shape of the cross. That cross carries within it an entire story and the foundation of human hope. It is the story of loss and gain, of the incarnation of the truly good one, his glorious life and triumphant defeat of death. The ashes are not just a reminder of our great failure; they remind us of God's victory over sin and death through the life, death, and resurrection of his Son.

In the garden after our first great disobedience, God did not give an immediate death sentence. He spared Adam and Eve, and he clothed them (Genesis 3:21). God's grace stayed his judgment. The human story would go forward. God also made a prophecy about the offspring of the woman, saying:

> I will put enmity
>> between you and the woman,
>> and between your offspring and hers;
> he will crush your head,
>> and you will strike his heel. (Genesis 3:15)

Christians have called this the *protoevangelium*, the first preaching of the gospel. Christ is the one born of woman who crushes the head of the serpent and brings about the salvation of humanity. The offspring of the serpent (the sons of evil) are at enmity with the sons of the light. The ashes on our forehead remind us that even as we continue our slow march toward death, we serve the one who has already defeated the enemy that stalks us.

THE PRAYER OF ASH WEDNESDAY

Lent is not about how angry God is with us for our sins. It is about a God who intervenes on our behalf to rescue us from our sins. This is why the collect for Lent in the Anglican tradition begins with these words: "Almighty and everlasting God, who hatest nothing that thou hast made, and dost forgive the sins of all those who are penitent."[1] The focus on penitence, fasting, and confession can lead us to believe that God needs to be appeased by us or that he will accept only a groveling and miserable humanity. Behind that false belief is the idea that a life of sin is better than life with God. The only downside is that sin brings judgment. In this view, the Christian is one who has reluctantly given up their sins to avoid judgment.

But this is not so. Life with God contains the good, the true, and the beautiful. God's call to repentance is a call to give up those things that can bring only death. Ash Wednesday calls us to remember death, and by calling us to remember death it calls us to remember what causes death: sin and rebellion. By forcing us to remember our sin, it helps us realize that, at bottom, our sins are lies about the true source of joy.

There's a reason the second part of that first collect of Ash Wednesday focuses on contrition: "Create and make in us new and contrite hearts, that we, worthily lamenting our sins and acknowledging our wretchedness, may obtain of thee, the God of all mercy, perfect remission and forgiveness, through Jesus Christ our Lord. Amen."[2] Contrition is about recognizing that our sins are just that—means by which we have fallen short of the glory of God. We cannot run from them until we recognize the danger they pose to our spiritual, emotional, and physical well-being. This is not something we can do by ourselves. As humans we too easily believe the lies sin tells us. That is why God must create in us new and contrite hearts. The feeling of sorrow for our sins is itself a grace.

The glorious thing about this collect, and all the prayers of Lent, is that they presume a loss of zeal. Over time we get comfortable in our sins. They become a part of who we are, a portion of the spiritual architecture of our lives. They are a limp we get used to walking with. Ash Wednesday (and Lent) is a call to remember our first love, the pursuit of holiness that may have marked the first years of our journey with God. Sin must become repulsive again. We need new hearts set aflame with love for God.

The logic of this prayer is not strictly soteriological. It's true that, in the end, God will forgive us of all kinds of sins of which we are unaware. Grace will triumph. But this prayer shows us we cannot be healed of sins we refuse to acknowledge. There is no greater joy or relief than to know we are forgiven by God. The first step in receiving that forgiveness is seeing our sins for what they are. In order to do that, we need hearts that are made new over and over again, because untended our hearts grow cold and unresponsive. We need the help of the Holy Spirit to show us the ways we have failed.

Lent, then, is about facing our failures. But we do not encounter a God who begrudgingly forgives our sins despite his better judgment. The apostle Paul says God is "rich in mercy" (Ephesians 2:4). This phrase evokes the divine name God revealed to Moses when he asked to see God's glory. God told Moses he was "the LORD, the LORD, the compassionate and gracious God, slow to anger, abounding in love and faithfulness" (Exodus 34:6). Instead of becoming a source of despair, our sin becomes the arena of God's glory. He doesn't have barely enough grace to forgive us. He is rich in the stuff; it overflows from his very nature. Ash Wednesday invites an introspection that leads to an acknowledgment of our sin that collides with an explosion of God's grace. No step in this process can be skipped.

THE SCRIPTURES OF ASH WEDNESDAY

Traditionally Ash Wednesday has included a reading from Joel. To ward off God's judgment (described in Joel 2:1-2), the prophet calls on the people to fast:

> Blow the trumpet in Zion,
>   declare a holy fast,
>   call a sacred assembly.
> Gather the people,
>   consecrate the assembly;
> bring together the elders,

> gather the children,
>> those nursing at the breast.
> Let the bridegroom leave his room
>> and the bride her chamber.
> Let the priests, who minister before the LORD,
>> weep between the portico and the altar.
> Let them say, "Spare your people, LORD.
>> Do not make your inheritance an object of scorn,
>> a byword among the nations.
> Why should they say among the peoples,
>> 'Where is their God?'" (Joel 2:15-17)

Joel's hope is not in the fast itself but in God's character as the one who is "gracious and compassionate" (Joel 2:13). In other words, Joel says that if Israel is destroyed, God's purposes and ability to fulfill his promises will be called into question. Therefore God must forgive the people. Fasting, then, is not about us earning God's forgiveness; it is about reminding ourselves through our fasting of our radical dependence on God. The fasting that begins with Ash Wednesday is caught up in the process of remembering our sins.

But it would be wrong to sidestep the reality of God's judgment that hangs over Ash Wednesday, Lent, and fasting. Yes, God is gracious to us. But beneath that statement about grace is a reminder of what sin is. Sin is rebellion against God, and that rebellion brings judgment. Lent demands that we remember that the day of the Lord (to steal the phrase from Joel) is "a day of darkness and gloom, a day of clouds and thick darkness."

It is good news that God judges sin, because sin harms both individuals and societies. The sins of greed and lust lead to the exploitation of women, children, and the vulnerable. The sin of racism leads to the harm of Black and Brown people in this country. The sins of arrogance and pride put us above our fellow humans. The sin of idolatry gives our hearts over to something other than our Creator. The sins of gossip and slander create lies that destroy lives and communities. God is gracious, but if we find ourselves caught up in the multitude of sins that lead to the harm of ourselves and others, we are on the wrong side of God, and that is a dangerous place to be. Lent reminds us of our danger.

The Gospel reading for Ash Wednesday highlights Jesus' own teaching about fasting and charity:

> Be careful not to practice your righteousness in front of others to be seen by them. If you do, you will have no reward from your Father in heaven.

So when you give to the needy, do not announce it with trumpets, as the hypocrites do in the synagogues and on the streets, to be honored by others. Truly I tell you, they have received their reward in full. But when you give to the needy, do not let your left hand know what your right hand is doing, so that your giving may be in secret. Then your Father, who sees what is done in secret, will reward you.

And when you pray, do not be like the hypocrites, for they love to pray standing in the synagogues and on the street corners to be seen by others. Truly I tell you, they have received their reward in full. But when you pray, go into your room, close the door and pray to your Father, who is unseen. Then your Father, who sees what is done in secret, will reward you. (Matthew 6:1-6)

Jesus highlights the dangers of fasting and other ceremonies that surround repentance. Before we begin this season, we must remember who it is for. The potential for self-deception is high. Any season of fasting or charity can turn into religion as performance instead of a service offered to God. I know some who look at the pomp and ceremony of liturgical churches, with our ashes on our heads visibly setting us apart, and see in us a violation of Jesus' commands. We should be fasting in secret. How can we reconcile a secret fast with a public Lent?

Those who engage in a season of fasting must take this criticism seriously. Isaiah too speaks about fasting for show. In his day the people fasted, but God seemed to pay no attention (see Isaiah 58:2-3). Isaiah says God isn't paying attention because the people are exploiting their workers and engaging in violent behavior during their religious fasts (Isaiah 58:4). The ritual of fasting hasn't touched them as persons. It hasn't led to a change in their lives. The prophet tells the people there is a kind of fast that God honors:

> To loose the chains of injustice
>> and untie the cords of the yoke,
> to set the oppressed free
>> and break every yoke . . .
> to share your food with the hungry
>> and to provide the poor wanderer with shelter.
>>> (Isaiah 58:6-7)

Isaiah doesn't condemn the people for engaging in public acts of repentance. There are numerous accounts of public penance in the Bible. The people of Nineveh covered themselves in sackcloth and ashes and fasted in response to the preaching of Jonah. The problem isn't that it is public; the problem is that it is *for* the public. Isaiah and Jesus make points that are much more subtle than we give them credit for. Both speak to the human heart, and getting to the bottom of its mystery is complicated. Any act can be directed toward God or other people. Jesus calls on us to examine our motives. If the problem is with our hearts, merely avoiding rituals won't save us from danger. We can make a show of *not* fasting or engaging in public acts of charity because we want people to know we are not like the legalists who do such things. In other words, there is no safe place to hide from the possibility of self-deception.

Nonetheless, discretion matters. Part of the discretion we display during Lent is trusting that rewards from God may be invisible. If we make a show before people, they reward us with respect and status. Rewards from God are designed to make us into people whose lives reflect him in the world. So, yes, we mark our heads with ashes— public shows of piety are not in themselves evil. But we must guard our motivations and do most of our spiritual work in private, because the privacy of those acts reveals (if only to us) our dependence on God.

The private acts Jesus calls for include acts of mercy toward the needy. In much the same way, Jesus' first sermon recorded in the Gospel of Luke highlights God's concern for those who experience injustice (Luke 4:16-30). Ash Wednesday, then, reminds us of one of the things it is easy to forget during the course of our journey with God: the stepped-on people of the world. They are the people whom Black theologian Howard Thurman called "the disinherited," those with their backs against the wall. Our journey toward God over the forty days of Lent includes a journey toward the suffering, because that is one place where God can be found (Matthew 25:34-46). Lent is not merely about extended reflections on our own mortality. It's a chance to open our lives and hearts to the pains of the world in imitation of our Lord, who looked with compassion on those with spiritual and material needs.

ASH WEDNESDAY: A LITANY THAT TRANSCENDS OUR MOMENT

Another distinctive element in the Anglican Ash Wednesday service is something modern prayer books call the "Litany of Penitence." A litany can simply be a list, like a litany of complaints. In church context, it refers to a series of prayers, often with a congregational response. The Litany of Penitence focuses on areas of sin we confess together at the beginning of Lent. It doesn't mean we are necessarily guilty of all these sins in the moment, but that at certain points in the year (day, week, month) we have failed in a wide variety of ways. The Litany of Penitence articulates the corporate failure of the church, and all our individual failures are caught up in that failure. It is an opportunity to examine ourselves.

The thing I love about this litany is that it transcends our current culture wars. Some Christians are highly focused on issues of justice. They love it when the litany says, "For our blindness to human need and suffering, and our indifference to injustice and cruelty; Accept our repentance, Lord."[3] This is a clear lament for the ways we allow structural injustices to linger because we are indifferent. This is well and good, but the litany isn't finished. It also speaks to personal holiness: "Our self-indulgent appetites and ways, and our exploitation of other people, We confess to you, Lord."[4] According to the liturgy, holiness matters. The litany also recognizes that we have failed in our devotion to God: "Our negligence in prayer and worship, and our failure to commend the faith that is in us, We confess to you, Lord."[5]

The litany doesn't condemn our ideological opponents and leave us feeling vindicated. A love for justice absent a love for God is empty. A love for God absent concern for our neighbors is a false witness. Love for God that doesn't pursue holiness misunderstands the freedom from sin inherent in the gospel.

The Litany of Penitence is an opportunity to meet ourselves and stop being dishonest about the things we have done. As an example, I like to lie about my physical condition. I find the friendliest mirror and the most generous lighting. But to find the truth, I step on the scale and see where I really am. The Litany of Penitence is a good scale that analyzes our spiritual fitness, not for the sake of condemnation, but so we know which areas need the most work.

THE JOURNEY BEGINS

Ash Wednesday is not a beginning, properly speaking. Even if, like the ancient converts to the faith, you're entering Lent as a preparation for baptism—you've heard the good news and decided to answer God's call—Lent is nonetheless an opportunity to reflect on the beginning of your life with God. For everyone else it is a chance to renew our commitment to Jesus.

In either case, Ash Wednesday's focus on grace and repentance is a gift to us. But it is not the only gift Lent has to offer. In chapter two we'll consider other rituals and spiritual practices that mark the season.

What Do These Things Mean?

The Rituals of Lent

When in the future your child asks you, "What
does this mean?" you shall answer . . .

Exodus 13:14 NRSV

As I said earlier, my encounter with liturgical spirituality began during the season of Lent. For that reason it has always been precious to me. I was in college at the University of the South (Sewanee). I had been raised in the Black Baptist tradition. I was not a disgruntled or unhappy Baptist. My Black church taught me the Scriptures. My Sunday school teachers and Bible study leaders told me we served a God of justice who cared about the oppressed. The deacons reminded me week in and week out that I could be whatever God called me to be. My pastor pleaded with us Sunday after Sunday to be reconciled to God and live for Christ. The men and women of the congregation had a clear vision of the kingdom of God, a world in which Christ's reign over a broken and divided world was a source of hope.

There was no recognized hole in my spiritual life. There was no trauma I was trying to escape. But today I find myself participating in traditions radically different from my own, with rituals that were once alien to me. This chapter is an attempt to explain how adding these spiritual habits has enriched my walk with God.

I don't remember hearing the word *Lent* growing up. As best I can recall, the liturgical calendar of our Baptist church consisted of Watch Night, Christmas, Mother's Day, pastor's anniversary, Psalm Sunday, and Easter. The only rituals I remember were roses on Mother's Day, palms on Palm Sunday, and a new suit for Easter.

During my senior year in college I was having some car trouble, which made it impossible for me to make my weekly trips to the church of my youth (my hometown of Huntsville, Alabama, is about an hour's drive from Sewanee, Tennessee). So I found myself attending the Episcopal chapel on campus. My first experience of liturgical worship was one of bewilderment. But over time, weekly Communion, along with the creeds, confessions, and prayers, began to stir something in me.

I realized that as much as I loved my Baptist church, it had not given me all the spiritual practices I needed to build a life. It had told me to read my Bible and go to church every Sunday. If I was really devout, I would go to Sunday school before church and midweek Bible study. But in the liturgy and the liturgical year I found a way of inhabiting and reflecting more intentionally on elements of Christian life and practice. I found that the liturgy helped me deepen and expand, not undo, the faith I'd been taught. It was a wonderful tool of discipleship. In the church year I found a life before God that I could pass on to my wife and kids. I did not have either at the time, but a man can dream, can't he?

FASTING

The best-known part of Lent is fasting. As we discussed in chapter one, the practice of fasting has varied across time and different parts of the church. Saint John Chrysostom said,

There are those who rival one another in fasting and show a marvelous emulation in it; indeed some who spend two whole days without food; and others who, rejecting from their tables not only the use of wine and of oil and of every dish, taking only bread and water, persevere in this practice during the whole of Lent.[1]

During my first Lent I was something of a zealot. I had never fasted and wanted to "do it right." I decided to give up meat for the entirety of Lent. I also did a total fast on Fridays, except for liquids. I have not done this again since—not because it was too difficult, but because I realized it had become about achievement and not my life before God. The purpose of fasting is to remind us that "One does not live by bread alone, but by every word that comes from the mouth of God" (Matthew 4:4 NRSV). Fasting wasn't supposed to be something I achieved but a reminder of my need for God's provision.

Another danger I saw in myself as the years went by was to turn Lent into a sanctified excuse to get into shape. Gluttony—seeking solace in food rather than God—is a real temptation. At the same time, in a society that hypersexualizes human persons and treats the perfection of the body as our defining virtue, the gift of the human body can become an idol. Therefore we must be careful that we are fasting to glorify God and not to win fleeting acclaim for our figure.

I am intentional about my fasts now. It's not about finding the biggest possible sacrifice. It's about examining the idols in myself and discerning the best way to tear them down. I also try to link sacrifices to goals for spiritual growth. If I decide to forgo coffee, the desire for coffee inevitably arises in my caffeine-deprived soul, so I use that opportunity to pray for patience or self-control.

Churches differ on how to count fasting days. In much of the Western Christian tradition, Sunday is a day of celebration and the Lenten fasts are not observed.

During my first Lent I kept up my Lenten observance throughout the entire season, including Sundays. In my enthusiasm I considered taking Sundays off too easy. Now I realize the wisdom the church offered me. If the purpose of a fast isn't to show God how much we are willing to suffer, then the Sunday exception makes sense. Sundays celebrate the victory of the bridegroom and his presence among us in the bread and wine. It's proper that Sundays be occasions of feasting. It's why throughout church history every Friday (even outside of Lent) has been an occasion for fasting of some kind, in remembrance of his passion. Every week is a mini liturgical experience with feasts, fasts, and even saints.

In some corners of the Anglican tradition only two days of complete fasting from food are encouraged: Ash Wednesday and Good Friday. Even then it is not a rule, it is simply recommended. For the rest of Lent and throughout our Christian lives, we trust individuals in conversation with their pastors and spiritual directors to discern the best ways to fast. We might choose to abstain from a certain food or practice as an offering to God. We might include total fasts, or fasts from certain meals. It doesn't matter what we do, but that we do it to God's glory.

STUDY

A healthy Lent is not merely about eating less chocolate; it's about remembering that we live by God's own words recorded in the Scriptures. But what does this look like practically? I like to set goals for myself that require intention without being overwhelming. I want to be able to dig deep into the Scriptures and reflect, instead of force-feeding myself texts I have little time to digest.

There are eighty-nine chapters in the four Gospels. Reading a little more than two chapters a day during Lent allows me to read through the Gospels by Easter. The same could be done with the thirteen letters of Paul, which total eighty-seven chapters. The rest of the New Testament consists of fifty-nine chapters, which could also be completed easily during the season. It would be simple, then, over the course of three Lenten seasons, to become highly familiar with the texts of the New Testament without the guilt that arises from excessive ambition, burnout, and failure.

RENEWAL

> I hold this against you: You have forsaken the love you had at first. (Revelation 2:4)

The church has also used the season of Lent to renew spiritual practices that have fallen away over the course of the year. In other words, Lent is not just about letting go of vices, but adding or recovering aspects of Christian faith and practice.

We engage in more liturgical practices during Lent than we do in any other period of the liturgical year. There are more recommended services, devotions, and practices in

Lent than, for example, Advent or Eastertide. This can be dangerous if we turn the season into an opportunity to store up extra merit in a spiritual bank account that we can slowly deplete over the rest of the year.

But it's also true that our relationship with God is like all other great loves. There are peaks and valleys. The fervency of young love gives way to the stability of lifelong commitment. In a marriage, it's easy to begin to take our spouse for granted along the way—the nights out and acts of kindness can give way to presumption and self-interest. There's a reason churches encourage the periodic renewal of marital vows. Likewise, clergy are required to renew their ordination vows annually. The whole church renews its baptismal vows whenever there is a baptism. We need constant recommitments.

Along the path of our lifelong spiritual journey it's easy to stop reading our Bibles and saying our prayers. We replace concern for the disinherited with competition with other inherited folks. Our focus turns from caring for the penniless to outdoing those whose coffers are full. Lent is about recovery, and recovery includes the Scriptures, prayer, the Eucharist—and works of charity.

CHARITY AND SOCIAL JUSTICE

The link between charity, social justice, and Lent is less well known than some other practices of the season, so let's engage in a little exposition. Christian charity is an enacted parable of the gospel. From God's perspective, all of us are needy, no matter how rich or powerful. We all need salvation and healing. So when we help the suffering we are imitating our Savior.

Charity also helps us resist the hierarchy that exists in a world without God. Societies tend to value people basely solely on their usefulness. Those without resources are often tossed away. We speed past them on the way to our jobs, vacations, and leisure pretending we do not see. But Christians serve a God who sees, so we must stop and see too. Once we see, we cannot close our hearts to help. Christian charity is a recovery of the imitation of Christ's ministry of healing as a sign of the coming kingdom. It does not replace the need for teaching about the Christian faith; it is another form of it.

While acts of charity are important, they do not always get at the root causes of our neighbors' suffering. It's great to provide meals for the homeless, but it's also necessary to ask how they became homeless in the first place. We are wrapped up in structures and societies that sin against and exploit individuals. To engage in justice work during Lent is to remember that we look for a city whose builder and maker is God.

While we do not fool ourselves into believing we can establish God's kingdom on earth before his second coming, we contend for justice as a way of bearing witness to the fact that our present experience is not the kingdom. Complacency with our personal sins is a danger, but so is accepting the sinfulness of the world as an unchangeable reality. Yes, the full work of transformation awaits the coming of Jesus, but there is still work to do here and now.

Confession

> But who can detect their errors?
> Clear me from hidden faults. (Psalm 19:12 NRSV)

If there was one thing I mocked Roman Catholics about for years (as far I thought about them at all), it was the practice of confession. Why go to a priest when you could go directly to God and receive forgiveness? I told myself there was only one mediator between God and man: Jesus Christ.

I have no desire to relitigate the controversies of the Reformation. But I will speak about how I changed my mind on confession and how it relates to the season of Lent.

The best explanation I can offer comes from Thomas Cranmer's exhortation that precedes the Communion service in the Book of Common Prayer. He begins by drawing on Paul's admonition in 1 Corinthians 11:27-33 that we take seriously the Lord's Supper lest we incur judgment. He encourages the Christian to "examine your life and conduct by the rule of God's commandments, and in whatsoever ye shall perceive yourselves to have offended, either by will, word, or deed, there to bewail your own sinfulness, and to confess yourselves to almighty God, with full purpose of amendment of life."[2] This seems pretty straightforward. Confess your sins to God. Then he says, "If there be any of you who by this means cannot quiet his own conscience . . . let him come to me, or to some other discreet and learned minister of God's word, and open his grief."[3] According to Cranmer, the Christian does this for the "quieting of his conscience and removing of all scruple and doubtfulness."[4]

Yes, we should confess our sins to God, but Cranmer points to benefits of confessing to clergy: it satisfies our conscience and removes all doubt. There is a world of difference between knowing intellectually that we are forgiven by God and experiencing the spiritual and emotional freedom that comes alongside the intellectual acknowledgment.

Clergy are not God. We do not have the power to forgive sins. But we have been given the task of preaching, teaching, leading, and disciplining the churches we lead. Most churches examine clergy before they ordain them, making sure they have the character and spiritual maturity to do that work. Clergy remain human, and we fall and sin like everyone else. In healthy systems, clergy are held accountable for their misdeeds. Nonetheless, churches have discerned a calling for the clergy to serve God's people by leading them. Therefore, when clergy say to people, "God forgives you," we speak on behalf of the church that has called us to this work.

It is true that James tells us to confess our sins to one another, and he doesn't say it has to be to clergy (James 5:16). That is good and well. But there is also value in bringing the things that concern us to those whose judgment has been assessed by the wider church. These truths can sit alongside one another. They don't have to be in competition. We confess to God, one another, and to clergy. Sometimes we need someone with spiritual authority to remind us of God's grace when our consciences are in trouble.

The diocese in which I was ordained requires future clergy to do a life confession before their ordination. I was terrified that if the priest knew about the foolishness of my youth or the dumb decisions I had made, I wouldn't be forgiven. I realized that anxiety and a troubled conscience had been with me for years. I was encouraged to write these things down so I wouldn't forget anything.

Surprisingly, it didn't take much space to write down my sins. It became clear as I reflected on my life that I often did the same things over and over, with a variation of time and circumstance. I came into the office with my sins written on yellow notebook paper. I sat facing the priest and we talked it through. The confession part went much more quickly than I expected. The priest then gave me some advice on ways I could pursue God more faithfully. It was like going to a spiritual doctor, listing my symptoms, and receiving the medicine.

One thing that sticks with me from that day is what the priest did with that yellow sheet of paper. He pulled up a metal basket next to us. He then took the paper that held my sins and lit it on fire, dropping the flaming paper into the bucket. He said, "The Lord has put away all your sins."

I felt more free in that moment than I had for years. Since then, confession has become a gift.

It is the custom in many Christian traditions to give a confession during the season of Lent. If this season is about renewing our spiritual lives, then it makes sense to take advantage of the sacrament of confession.

Confession is helpful because it involves examining our spiritual life in an intentional manner. Many serious Christians, realizing they are stuck in sin, will confess it to themselves or others and try to change. But there is also a host of sins of which we are unaware. Part of the preparation for confession is an in-depth self-examination. There are multiple ways to go about this, but one of the most common approaches is to use Scripture. We go through the Ten Commandments and the Sermon on the Mount and ask ourselves if we are in violation of the principles contained in these Scriptures in thought, word, or deed.

The old devotional books also have lists of vices for us to consider. For example, regarding snobbery, the Saint Augustine's Prayer Book wonders, "Have you been prideful over race, family, position, personality, education, skill, achievements, or possessions?" This is not a question

I often put to myself. It is good for me to reflect on such things—not so I can feel wicked, but so I might be healed.

Confession isn't about going to the priest to obtain a forgiveness not otherwise available. It is about God working through clergy to help us understand the forgiveness he offers and to discern together the best way to live our lives before God. We cannot be healed of what we refuse to acknowledge. So we examine ourselves in light of God's word for the sake of our healing and restoration.

STATIONS OF THE CROSS

We adore you, O Christ, and we bless you:
Because by your holy cross you have redeemed
the world.[5]

Another common practice of Lent is the Stations of the Cross service. The Stations of the Cross most likely began in Jerusalem as Christians recounted Jesus' journey from the home of Pontius Pilate to Golgotha.[6] Today it is a service held in churches with prayers and readings at each station. The number of stations has varied throughout the centuries, but the church seems to have mostly settled on fourteen.

Churches vary in the use of the stations. Some hold a service only on Good Friday. Others hold a Stations of the Cross service every Friday during Lent. I prefer the latter, personally, because it gives me time and space to allow the different aspects of the journey to the cross speak as the Lord wills.

The fourteen Stations of the Cross are:

1. Jesus is condemned to death.

2. Jesus takes up his cross.

3. Jesus falls the first time.

4. Jesus meets his afflicted mother.

5. The cross is laid on Simon of Cyrene.

6. A woman wipes the face of Jesus.

7. Jesus falls a second time.

8. Jesus meets the women of Jerusalem.

9. Jesus falls a third time.

10. Jesus is stripped of his garments.

11. Jesus is nailed to the cross.

12. Jesus dies on the cross.

13. The body of Jesus is placed in the arms of his mother.

14. Jesus is laid in the tomb.[7]

The Stations of the Cross are a mix of pious legend (as in the story of Veronica at station six) and the biblical narrative (the account of Simon of Cyrene). That doesn't mean only the latter are important. There was so much going on during the last moments of Jesus' life that it is certain some events were not recorded. I consider the nonbiblical stations means by which we enter into the expansive scene of Jesus' final journey this side of death.

At each station there is a brief setting of the scene, followed by a prayer. Some traditional churches have pictures of the fourteen stations lining the sanctuary. During the service, you journey to each station, pausing to recite the prayer and meditate on its significance. One of the most moving stations is thirteen. It begins as they all do with the response:

> We adore you, O Christ, and we bless you
> Because by your holy cross you have redeemed
>   the world.

Central to the service is a sense of awe and celebration alongside melancholy. The cross of Christ is the means by which we find forgiveness, but that forgiveness is not without suffering. We worship Christ and adore the cross because it reveals that he loved us enough to suffer on our behalf. The cross is the place where tragedy is turned into joy. When the apostle Paul said he preached nothing except Christ and him crucified (1 Corinthians 2:2), it wasn't because Paul limited his proclamation to the bloody details of the crucifixion. It was because the cross and resurrection contain the whole world. All stories that matter have Golgotha as their climax.

The infancy narratives are especially poignant because we know that the baby born on Christmas will one day defeat death.

So we spend extra time during Lent pondering the cross because our hope buds from the wood of the blood-stained tree. But before we get to the joy of that tree, we must face its pain. Station thirteen includes the following collage of scriptural texts:

All you who pass by, behold and see if there is any sorrow like my sorrow. My eyes are spent with weeping; my soul is in tumult; my heart is poured out in grief because of the downfall of my people. "Do not call me Naomi (which means Pleasant), call me Mara (which means Bitter); for the Almighty has dealt very bitterly with me."[8]

Two tragedies are combined here, one national and one personal. There are elements of the Book of Lamentations and mourning over the fall of Jerusalem. There is also the dirge of Naomi and her mourning over the loss of her husband and sons. These are our pains. We weep over a world full of death and mayhem, even as we also lament the small and personal traumas of our own lives.

At this station Mary is depicted holding on to the dead body of Jesus. She is both weeping mother and one witnessing the death of Israel's hope. We are Mary. We must stare into this double-edged darkness before we can find our way toward hope. The season calls on us to confront the true scope of the human dilemma writ small and large. The world is dark and full of evil. We are a people who know weeping. We know weeping for our sins and tragedies as well as the sins of the world.

It's easy to store away the benefits of the cross. The benefits of forgiveness can become background noise in a life filled with complacency. We need to remember the danger. We need to recall what Christ did to reconcile us to himself. Our hearts must be broken for our sins. We must walk alongside him to the mount of our redemption, shedding our compromises and transgressions along the way.

Encountering Grace

> The work of God is this: to believe in the one he has
> sent. (John 6:29)

Jesus has done too much for us to believe we can ever earn God's favor. The abundant grace of God is the Christian's great comfort. Spiritual practices of fasting, prayer, Bible reading, special devotions, and works of justice do not lessen the work of Christ. Instead, these practices open up space to encounter the grace of God.

Like anything else of value, the spiritual disciplines require effort. The practices of Lent are meant to give guidance for growth. When the doctor prescribes medicine, the medicine is not the point; the point is the healing that comes through the medicine. These practices should not become burdens on the backs of Christians who already have a host of insecurities and traumas. Instead they should be received as family wisdom, insights into growing in the grace of God.

I have had Lenten seasons when I kept all the commitments I made at the beginning. I have also had times when the whole thing fell apart. In both situations, I have been overcome by the celebrations of Christ's passion and resurrection in Holy Week. The joy of the Lord is not a ticket to be purchased by our fasts. He is always good.

3

What We Have Received

The Prayers and Scriptures of Lent

For I received from the Lord what I also passed on to you.

1 Corinthians 11:23

As someone who came from outside the liturgical expressions of Christianity, I had a certain suspicion of the whole enterprise. I thought the liturgical tradition, with its vestments, rituals, rules, and customs, was the very thing Jesus had come to destroy. What God wanted, I intuited, was a broken and contrite heart. He owned the cattle on a thousand hills; he didn't need our formalized prayers and spiritual sacrifices.

The heroes in my mind were characters like David, who danced informally before God (2 Samuel 6:14), and the prophets, whose ministry was led from start to finish by the Spirit (1 Kings 18:12). The liturgical life seemed, from the outside, to stifle the Spirit. In my developing religious sensibilities, inherited from the Free Church Protestantism of my youth, the legalists Paul battled in Galatia had morphed into modern ritualistic Christians. Jesus wanted prayers from my heart that revealed my own wrestling with God, not the repeated words of those long dead. God was, of course, on the side of the informalists and against the formalists. In the language that became omnipresent during my college years, it wasn't about religion but relationship. Religion was shorthand for any ritual activity with which I was uncomfortable.

Here in these pages, I want to approach the liturgy from a different perspective. I do not wish to engage in debates about particular texts of the Bible. I want instead to zoom out and look at the nature of the Old and New Testaments themselves. I want to press in on the method by which God forms a people. When God revealed himself to a spiritually malnourished group who needed to be taught the things required for holiness, what did he do? How did God do it?

He gave his people rituals. He gave them feasts tied to certain parts of the year and a system of sacrifice to teach his ways to coming generations:

> When in the future your child asks you, "What does this mean?" you shall answer, "By strength of hand the Lord brought us out of Egypt, from the house of slavery. When Pharaoh stubbornly refused to let us go, the Lord killed all the firstborn in the land of Egypt, from human firstborn to the firstborn of animals. Therefore I sacrifice to the Lord every male that first opens the womb, but every firstborn of my sons I redeem." (Exodus 13:14-15 NRSV)

Established prayers and actions pass on the faith, not as magic activities that contain meaning in themselves, but as occasions for remembering. And these rituals are not in conflict with deeply emotive experiences of God. Every psalm and song, every word of prayer and lament in the Old Testament, was written by Jewish people steeped in the rituals of Israel. The fact of the deeply personal relationship with God demonstrated in the Psalms, Jeremiah, and Isaiah gives lie to the idea that God only values informality.

Some might be tempted to ask, didn't Jesus come to do away with all those rituals to worship in spirit and in truth (John 4:24)? Wasn't the law a shadow of things to come (Colossians 2:17)? Well, sort of. The Old Testament sacrificial and liturgical system pointed toward Christ as the fulfillment of the law. Referring to the law as a shadow speaks to its fulfillment in Christ. The reference to "shadows" does not speak to ritual as a means of spiritual formation. It does not eliminate the possibility that ritual can be a means of encountering the living God.

Stories and rituals pass on understanding. Jesus knew this. During his last night with his disciples he did not have them memorize a position paper on the meaning of the atonement; he gave them a meal—a ritual with set words and actions that immediately entered the life of the early church. This why Paul can say, "I received from the Lord what I also passed on to you: The Lord Jesus, on the night he was betrayed, took bread . . . " (1 Corinthians 11:23). Paul refers to central aspects of Christian doctrine, like the resurrection and ritual activities, as things he received (1 Corinthians 11:23; 15:1-3). Both the ritual piety and the apostolic doctrines are part of our inheritance as Christians.

Our discussion does not mean that ritual or even the Lord's Supper is limited to a pedagogical technique. Christians throughout the centuries have maintained that in and through things like the bread and wine of the Eucharist, God comes to meet us. Christ doesn't just teach us about himself in the Eucharist; he comes to us and nourishes the weary believer. We can have both. Ritual is both a means of spiritual formation (we learn through repetition) and an encounter (God meets us in the act of worship and praise in the liturgy).

What does any of this have to do with Lent and its prayers? The set prayers of Lent are not a limitation on Christian devotion. They do not stand in the way of offering our own heartfelt cries to God. They are a way of accepting that we are not the first ones to encounter the God who has tossed our lives into a glorious confusion. Others have left a testimony. Their witness deserves to be heard. It would be impossible to trace all the Lenten prayers across Christian traditions; instead I will focus on the collects of the Anglican tradition and consider some scriptural texts often associated with the season.

PRAYER FOR THE FIRST WEEK OF LENT

> Almighty God, whose blessed Son was led by the
> Spirit to be tempted of Satan: Make speed to help
> thy servants who are assaulted by manifold tempta-
> tions; and, as thou knowest their several infirmities,
> let each one find thee mighty to save; through Jesus
> Christ thy Son our Lord, who liveth and reigneth
> with thee and the Holy Spirit, one God, now and for
> ever. Amen.[1]

The First Sunday of Lent often includes a reading of Jesus'
temptation in the wilderness by Satan. It occurs in all the
Synoptic Gospels with varying levels of detail (Matthew
4:1-11; Mark 1:12-13; Luke 4:1-13). On the surface this
could be dismissed as mere proof texting: Jesus fasted
forty days and Lent lasts forty days. But there is more
going on here, as the prayer makes clear.

The question at the core of all Christian hope is, precisely, what is the nature of the God to whom we swear
allegiance? We serve a God who has come among us in
the person of his Son. The author of Hebrews makes this
plain when he says, "For we do not have a high priest who
is unable to empathize with our weaknesses, but we have

one who has been tempted in every way, just as we are—yet he did not sin" (Hebrews 4:15). Jesus knows how to minister to us because he was tempted like we are tempted, but with one crucial difference. He did not sin.

This brings us back to the various depictions of Jesus' victory over Satan in the wilderness. The Gospels show that in these early years of his ministry, Jesus embodies the experiences of Israel. He comes up out the Jordan River just as Israel passed through the Red Sea. He goes into the wilderness for forty days just as Israel spent forty years in the wilderness. The major difference, which both the author of Hebrews and the Gospel writers recognize, is that Jesus succeeds were the Israelites failed. While Israel took up idols during its sojourn in the wilderness, Jesus takes up the Scriptures, quoting Deuteronomy three times in reply to the temptations Satan presents him.

Here at the start of our Lenten journey, we are reminded of the source of our hope. We follow Jesus because he succeeded where we failed. He resisted the temptations that have conquered us all. He kept the fast. Our fasts have no power in and of themselves to earn God's favor. Instead, they are a way of entering into communion with Jesus, whose faithfulness secures our present and future life with God.

This prayer makes an important statement about the human condition. It says we are "assaulted by many temptations." We live our Christian lives in community. We worship together, read our Bibles together, and pray for one another. But no other human knows the exact nature of the battles we face every day. We are surrounded by a host of temptations: greed, lust, dishonesty, coveting, anger, cruelty. No one sees the grievances and distortions we carry within us. But this prayer reminds us that God knows us. He doesn't know our sins only in the general sense of being aware of the general brokenness of humanity. He is familiar with each and every failure. He sees our weaknesses. He knows the sins that entice us more than others. And because he is cognizant of our weaknesses, he can tell us exactly what we need to do to be healed.

But it has to be a healing we want. If we're honest, we sin, at least initially, because we enjoy it. Before the darkness rises and we see the wreckage we've caused, we convince ourselves that a little jaunt across the moral boundaries God has placed around us is harmless. It's only when sin has its grasp firmly established that it unsheathes its claws.

When we find ourselves trapped, it is only Jesus who is both mighty to save and gentle enough to restore without breaking us. Restoration is possible, but it will hurt, because removing claws is always painful.

Like most collects, this prayer ends with a trinitarian formula. We live in the presence of the triune God who created all things and will see them to their proper end. This is good news, because that God is gracious and loves humankind.

PRAYER FOR THE SECOND WEEK OF LENT

> O God, whose glory it is always to have mercy: Be gracious to all who have gone astray from thy ways, and bring them again with penitent hearts and steadfast faith to embrace and hold fast the unchangeable truth of thy Word, Jesus Christ thy Son; who with thee and the Holy Spirit liveth and reigneth, one God, for ever and ever. Amen.[2]

This prayer reminds us that God's greatest glory comes not in the crushing of all opposition or immediate destruction of the disobedient. God is glorified through his mercy. To read the Bible well is to become acquainted with God's patience. Beginning in the garden and running through the entire history of Israel, we see God graciously calling a wayward people to himself. The image of Christ as the good shepherd who seeks lost sheep has always been a comfort because it illustrates this aspect of God's character; he always comes for us. Lent involves us recognizing that he indeed has to seek us out because we get lost from time to time. This prayer asks God to do what he has already shown himself eager to accomplish: *God, please come for us, our friends, our neighbors, and our family members when we stray from the way of life you have marked out for us in your Son.*

A common reading from the second week of Lent is 1 Thessalonians 4:1-8. In it, Paul reminds the Christian of the way of life we learned from Jesus, which includes holiness, having control of our own body, and not being consumed by lust or sexual immorality. Paul calls on the church to not "take advantage of a brother or sister" (1 Thessalonians 4:6). Here Paul makes it plain that our sins (sexual and otherwise) do not merely damage us; they spill into the lives of others. If we have gone astray from God in a way that harms ourselves and others, this prayer reminds us that it's never too late to repent and return and that God is gracious and will forgive us.

What we are tempted to call a list of vices in 1 Thessalonians 4:1-8 is in fact something else. It is a list of hindrances. This is not just a list of things we do wrong. They are things that get in the way of our calling. First Thessalonians 4:7 says, "God did not call us to be impure, but to live a holy life." It is a vision of life with God that compels us to put aside the sins that get in the way. This prayer together with this reading opens up a chance for reflection. Which sins have gotten in the way of our callings?

Prayer for the Third Week of Lent

Almighty God, who seest that we have no power of ourselves to help ourselves: Keep us both outwardly in our bodies and inwardly in our souls, that we may be defended from all adversities which may happen to the body, and from all evil thoughts which may assault and hurt the soul; through Jesus Christ our Lord, who liveth and reigneth with thee and the Holy Spirit, one God, for ever and ever. Amen.[3]

I remember sitting next to my oldest son when he was much smaller, waiting patiently for him to finish tying his shoes. He was just beginning to master the loops and knots. With his still-developing manual dexterity, there were many starts and stops. We both knew I could do the work much faster and we could be on our way. We also both knew this wasn't a possibility. He had to do it himself.

Part of being a parent is preparing our children for independence. We hope they outgrow us and become whatever it is God has called them to be. We want them to fly the coop and hopefully float farther and higher than we ever did.

But we do not outgrow God. We never arrive at a place where we are able to "take it from here." We are not deists who believe that God set our spiritual lives in motion and now sits back to see what we will do with ourselves. Instead we are like the hymnist who says,

I need Thee every hour,
Stay thou nearby;
Temptations lose their power
When thou art nigh.[4]

The third prayer in Lent reminds Christians of our deep need for a Savior: "We have no power in ourselves to help ourselves." Too often, Christians believe the lie that we have to dig down deep and discover in ourselves the strength and resolve to defeat our foes. Instead, we must realize that if we dig down to the bottom of ourselves, we'll find a wounded soul in need of healing.

Now let's not get it confused. This is not a claim that there is nothing good in any of us. We received the gift of being created in the image of God. That means all of us are capable of real acts of kindness and beauty. But two more things must be said. First, those moments of goodness and kindness have their origins in God. They are a gift from him, even if we don't acknowledge them as such. Second, the gift of being created in God's image, as precious as it is, is not enough. We need something more, something outside ourselves. We a need a power stronger than death.

Paul says we have it. He writes to the church in Ephesus, "I pray that the eyes of your heart may be enlightened in order that you may know the hope to which he has called you, the riches of his glorious inheritance in his holy people, and his incomparably great power for us who believe. That power is the same as the mighty strength he exerted when he raised Christ from the dead" (Ephesians 1:18-20). What hope do we have that the commitments we have made will withstand the trauma of the human experience? Both Paul and the prayer for the third week of Lent give the same answer: God's power.

What do we need this power to do? We know that at the last God will call our dead bodies to life to be with him forever. If that is all God did for us we would praise him for it. But God in his mercy has promised us more. During the third week of Lent we recall that our bodies and our souls are vulnerable. We can be harmed. We age and get sick.

In the old prayer books, the reading for the third Sunday of Lent comes from the first half of Ephesians chapter 5. In that section Paul lists the sins from which we need to flee: sexual immorality, foul language, greed, idolatry, and so on. This might strike us as the old legalism finding its way back into our lives to steal our joy. Instead we should see those sins as thieves of joy. This call to flee is a kindness, even when we don't experience it as such. Sometimes it's the shock of a truth plainly spoken that awakens us to how far we have fallen from the things of God.

I am glad prayers like this begin to make their appearance in the middle of Lent. By the time we make it to the third week, our initial enthusiasm has started to wane. The excitement of fasting and renewed commitment to God has started to waver. We are still too far from Easter to be excited about the celebratory end of the fast, and we are too far from the beginning to remember our initial repentance. We can't keep ourselves from straying without God's grace.

Much of the Christian life is found in this middle place, between initial joy and final consummation. It's precisely then that the compromises start to creep in.

This is why the spiritual disciplines are called "disciplines." We will not always be enthusiastic about following God. Some days, weeks, months, and even years, each step we take down the narrow path that leads to salvation feels like a chore. In those moments our hope is not in the fervency of our piety but in the reality of the thing on which we have placed our hopes. The tomb is empty. Death is conquered even when church is boring, the music middling, and the sermon uninspired. The tomb is empty even when whatever spiritual gain we might have achieved through our fasts pales in comparison to a double cheeseburger and a milkshake.

We keep the fast during the middle portions of Lent because our relationship with God is not an infatuation. Anyone who has remained a Christian over the long haul knows that commitment—not mere enthusiasm—is love fully matured.

Prayer for the Fourth Week of Lent

Gracious Father, whose blessed Son Jesus Christ came down from heaven to be the true bread which giveth life to the world: Evermore give us this bread, that he may live in us, and we in him; who liveth and reigneth with thee and the Holy Spirit, one God, now and for ever. Amen.[5]

If our desires cannot satisfy us, what can? What is sufficient to satiate our deep need for meaning, joy, and purpose?

The collect from the fourth Sunday of Lent invites us to consider Jesus' startling assertion that he is "the bread of life." This claim is taken from the sixth chapter of John's Gospel. The chapter begins with Jesus feeding the multitudes with five loaves of bread and two fish. This miracle leads the people to declare that Jesus is "the Prophet who is to come into the world" (John 6:14). We can't blame them for being wooed—the purpose of the miracle was to reveal Jesus to them—but they missed the point of it. The message they took (and the posture we might be tempted to adopt) is one in which God is useful only insomuch as he meets our material needs.

This is a God who is worthy of our time and attention only when he is blessing us. I do not want to undersell the material difference the gospel can make in the lives of believers. Nonetheless, it would be dishonest to claim that things always get easier when someone becomes a Christian. God doesn't guarantee us a new car, a better job, or a long-hoped-for spouse. In fact, sometimes becoming a Christian means you *lose* a job or find yourself outside a social circle you once called home. Depending on the part of the world you live in, it may even cost you your life.

This is why Jesus said, after the miracle of the loaves and fish,

> Very truly I tell you, you are looking for me, not because you saw the signs I performed but because you ate the loaves and had your fill. Do not work for food that spoils, but for food that endures to eternal life, which the Son of Man will give you. For on him God the Father has placed his seal of approval. (John 6:26-27)

If all we want from God is a full belly, our vision is too small. Both the food and the person who consumes it will pass away.

We must be careful, though. This can become a pathway toward complacency. We might be tempted to hear Jesus declaring the relative unimportance of material things, therefore we should see simply to the spiritual needs of the poor and not worry much about their physical requirements. We could take Jesus to mean that the poor need only the proclamation of the gospel.

Jesus does say he is more important than food that perishes, but he doesn't use that as an excuse for not helping the hungry or showing compassion to the needy. Instead, after he feeds the people, Jesus says he has more to offer than they can imagine. Jesus wants to give the hungry more, not less.

What is it then that Christianity offers? What do we have to give the world that it cannot acquire elsewhere? Or, to press the point more sharply, why do we stick with Jesus when we are hungry, sick, lonely, or sad? Why do we continue on when we lift our eyes and see a church compromised in so many ways? If Lent is about asking hard questions, then the question of "Why any of this at all?" must be answered not only annually but daily.

The answer Jesus gives in John's Gospel—which the prayer for the fourth week of Lent picks up on—is this: we receive Jesus. What makes the Christian special is we have the Messiah who has come to give life to the world.

We don't just get his death for our sins; we get the life he lived before he died, which gives his death meaning. We receive his defeat of death, which gives us hope. We get his instructions. As he told the crowd, we are all taught by God (John 6:45). It is in Christ that we encounter a vision of the human life large enough to satisfy all our longings; it is in the person of Christ that we encounter a God who demands our allegiance.

It may be too simple to put it this way, but some things must be stated as plainly as possible. We must set aside time to ponder the God we serve and remember the great privilege we have to be invited into his family. It is only when the light of Christ shines on our sins that we can see them for the small and petty things they are. We are not merely satisfied, as if Christ were a barely sufficient meal. He is a feast in the presence of our enemies.

PRAYER FOR THE FIFTH WEEK OF LENT

Almighty God, you alone can bring into order the unruly wills and affections of sinners: Grant your people grace to love what you command and desire what you promise; that, among the swift and varied changes of the world, our hearts may surely there be fixed where true joys are to be found; through Jesus Christ our Lord, who lives and reigns with you and the Holy Spirit, one God, now and for ever. Amen.[6]

But there is a problem, which the final collect before Holy Week makes plain. We don't always want to obey Jesus' commands. This is why the prayer asks God for "grace to love what you command and desire what you promise." This is a call to maturity. We must admit that sometimes after the music stops, the sermon ends, and the liturgy concludes, we still want to sin. Our wills and our hearts are, in the words of the hymn writer, "prone to wander." Sin jumps out at us unexpectedly. We have spent weeks in prayer and devotion. We go to church weekly, attend small groups, and take Eucharist regularly. Then in an instant we become surprisingly angry or cruel. We become self-centered or self-indulgent. We want to disobey simply because it appears to lead to happiness.

And it can appear as if God's commands stand in the way of that happiness. Don't get me wrong. We can understand intellectually why he commands what he does. We can know they are good for our souls, and not evil—but they are still commands. And we have become a people who are unused to limitations.

This prayer is a call for God to visit us with his power so we can see in those commands the joy they offer. We need to see honesty, kindness, goodness, and self-control as goods, not burdens. We need to see holiness as life and not the tamping down on things that bring us thrills. How do we do this? First, we must see the actual damage sin causes. We need to see marriages and families ripped apart by infidelity. We need to see the harm visited on the weak when the powerful take what they want. We need to see that all moral and spiritual bills eventually come due.

This requires the ability to see. The world is swift and changing. The pleasures it offers are fleeting. But if our hearts are fixed on the God who does not change, we can locate our joy where it will never be taken from us. God gives us the only joy that endures. It is joy that is not at the expense of others. It is joy that gives life to those around us instead of taking it away. We must understand that the life God offers is materially better in every sense of the word than the life the world gives us, because God is the one who created all things and has oriented reality toward the good, the true, and the beautiful. We must learn to see in the life he offers us the beauty he contains.

The reflections I have offered here are not the only way to make your way through the prayers and Scriptures of Lent. I hope I have shown that Lent is not about endless repetition of the fact that we are sinners. Instead, it offers us over and over the chance to see the beauty of life with God—a beauty that has been obscured by a multitude of compromises. Lent is a quieting of the soul and a lessening of distractions so we can again hear the voice of God. We hear that voice through the prayers the church has given us, not as restraints on our devotion but as an invitation to ponder again the things of God.

4

He Loved Us to the End

HOLY WEEK

Jesus knew that the hour had come for him to leave
this world and go to the Father. Having loved his own
who were in the world, he loved them to the end.

JOHN 13:1

Much of Lent is thematic. It doesn't try to squeeze the whole earthly life of Jesus into forty days. Instead, it gives us space to reflect on our life with God and to regain what may have been lost. For the convert, it is a preparation for a life with Christ that begins at baptism.

Holy Week is different. Here things do get a bit chronological. Palm Sunday, Maundy Thursday, Good Friday, and Holy Saturday all depict events from the last days of Jesus' earthly life. But the Scriptures infuse these events with deep meaning. There are the bare facts of the events themselves, but we also get insight into what these events mean for the life of the world.

Holy Week invites us to journey with Jesus and enter into the significance of these events, beginning with Palm Sunday.

Palm Sunday

All glory, laud, and honor
To thee, Redeemer, King,
To whom the lips of children
Made sweet hosannas ring.
Thou art the King of Israel,
Thou David's royal Son,
Who in the Lord's name comest
The King and Blessed One.[1]

At many churches Palm Sunday begins outside. The members of the congregation receive palm branches and repeat the shout of "Hosanna to the Son of David!" This portion of the service links our refrain to the cries of those who celebrated his entry into the city. But the service also displays an awareness of things unknown to anyone in Jerusalem but Jesus himself. We praise God "for the acts of love by which you have redeemed us through your Son Jesus Christ our Lord."[2] This act of love is the cross that awaits him on Golgotha. Both we and the crowds in Jerusalem laud him as the promised Son of David, but only those of us who follow him after his resurrection from the dead know the full shape of that Davidic kingship.

If discipleship is about following Jesus, then the invitation to walk with Jesus during his last week is a call to be formed by the journey. What do we learn through the Liturgy of the Palms? What do we discover that makes us better followers of Jesus? We tend to focus on the palm branch as the central image because it's so easy bring to life. We can buy palm branches in bulk. But the most important symbol of the day may have been the donkey. After all, it was the symbol Jesus chose.

In the biblical narrative the scene unfolds with Jesus on the outskirts of Jerusalem instructing his disciples to bring him a donkey to ride into the city. The Gospel writers make it clear that this royal gesture is a dramatic enactment of Zechariah 9:9. The section quoted in the Gospels says,

Do not be afraid, Daughter Zion;

see, your king is coming,

seated on a donkey's colt. (John 12:15)

The sign of the king of the universe coming on a donkey's colt has been fodder for many hymns, possibly the most famous being these lines:

Ride on, ride on in majesty!

In lowly pomp ride on to die.

Bow thy meek head to mortal pain;

Then take, O God, thy power and reign.[3]

Palm Sunday reveals Jesus' humility. He is not like other kings who enter cities atop war horses in celebration of bloody victory. He is the humble king who saves by dying for the sins of the world. Jesus' care for the lowly has long been a source of solace for oppressed people.[4] If we are going to follow Jesus, then we do not have to fight the way the world fights. We do not use their tools and means to get what we want. Palm Sunday challenges us to consider whether we have adopted the efficiency of force and cruelty instead of the way of Jesus. Stated differently, Jesus' life was not just a means of salvation; it was a way of being human.

Rejecting the way of violence extends beyond critiquing kings and war horses. It includes how we treat those we love and those we disdain. It extends to how we interact with our friends, family, children, and coworkers. Are we people of violence? Can we put aside that violence and follow Jesus into the city, knowing what love demands of us?

Palm Sunday is actually two events in one. Chronologically, it remembers Jesus' entry into Jerusalem. But during the service proper, it also recalls the crucifixion. It is customary to read Psalm 22, Isaiah 52:13–53:12, and one of the Synoptic accounts of Jesus' death on Palm Sunday. (John's account is usually reserved for Good Friday.) I have noticed that on this day it is not common to reflect extensively on atonement theories. In part this is logistics: the palm celebration at the beginning and the larger readings throughout tend to sap the energy of the congregation. There will also be an opportunity to discuss the meaning of Christ's death on Good Friday.

What are we to do, then, with the story of the crucifixion told on the same day we recall Jesus' entry into the city? I think this placement of the crucifixion story reminds us where all Christ's journeys eventually led. Every

Christian now exists on the other side of the crucifixion and resurrection. The whole of Jesus' story, from the first cries in the manger through the donkey ride into the city, has the cross in the background. These readings (without extensive commentary) also help us remember that the cross is not just something to discuss, interpret, and understand. It is a thing to behold. We must see the act of love set before us again and again. The crucifixion story bears repeating.

Maundy Thursday

> Almighty Father, whose dear Son, on the night before he suffered, instituted the Sacrament of his Body and Blood: Mercifully grant that we may receive it thankfully in remembrance of Jesus Christ our Lord, who in these holy mysteries gives us a pledge of eternal life.[5]

There are services associated with Monday through Wednesday of Holy Week, but the chronology of Jesus' last days picks up with Maundy Thursday. *Maundy* is an abbreviation of the Latin word *mandatum*, which means "command." It refers to the commandment Jesus gave his disciples: to love one another.

This service begins the holiest part of the Christian year, called the Easter Triduum. *Triduum* means a period of three days. In this case it is the three days of Maundy Thursday, Good Friday, and the Easter Vigil. We like to think of them as three separate services, but in point of fact, as we shall see, they are one.

Maundy Thursday remembers the Last Supper and the installation of the Eucharist. It also remembers Jesus' washing of the disciples' feet.

My life as a Baptist did not prepare me for much of the liturgical life, but I can say that I have washed more feet than any priest I know.[6] This is not because the Anglican churches I attended enthusiastically embraced Maundy Thursday—it's because I was raised in the Primitive Baptist Church. In that tradition, like most Baptist churches, we celebrated the Lord's Supper. But we added an additional element that I have not seen practiced monthly elsewhere. We washed each other's feet on the second Sunday of every month.

The service was simple. The congregation divided, with men on one side and women on the other. Then the deacons brought out bowl after bowl of water, along with enough towels to supply a summer pool party. New members to our church, unaware of this custom, did not pay attention to where they sat. They did not have information that was well known to long-time members of the congregation: you wash the feet of the person next to you.

Sitting next to one of the more "mature" members of the congregation was something of an adventure. Alabama summers are warm, and those church socks are not designed to absorb moisture. The young people in the congregation had an unspoken pact. On footwashing Sunday, we stuck together and made sure our feet and socks were pristine. Showers on Sunday mornings before church were a requirement. Come Sunday, we also agreed not to require excessive diligence in the washing department. A quick splash and rub were sufficient.

Nonetheless, there I sat, month after month, year after year, washing the feet of the young and the old, hearing the words of Jesus in the King's English:

> If I then, your Lord and Master, have washed your
>   feet; ye also ought to wash one another's feet.
> For I have given you an example, that ye should do
>   as I have done to you.
> Verily, verily, I say unto you, The servant is not
>   greater than his lord. (John 13:14-16 KJV)

I never learned to enjoy footwashing. I'm not sure joy was the intent. Service and mutual love are hard work. Sometimes we must grab sweaty feet and say to the person to whom those sweaty feet belong, "You are loved and valued, not just by your brothers and sisters in Christ, but more importantly by God." Footwashing was gospel work. It was not fun, but it was good.

It was not until I became aware of Maundy Thursday and Lent that I found out most Christians washed feet only once per year, and then it was all done by clergy. Initially, I liked the liturgical version much better. After all, who couldn't wash feet just once per year? Plus, most members were too shy to come forward for footwashing. So the clergy were willing to humble themselves, but the congregation thought such humility was not required. It was the best of both worlds: all the humility and none of the sacrifice.

But my Primitive Baptist past betrayed me. I knew from long experience that those Baptist footwashing services required a vulnerability many of us would rather avoid. But the very things we run from are what are needed to bring healing to our souls. Instead of receiving that healing, we make the same deal I made with my friends. If you put on your best socks on footwashing Sunday, I will do the same. If you pretend you do not need my help, I will pretend I do not need yours. We can fake it together.

But this is a lie. Maundy Thursday is about facing that deception. We need God's love and the love of the community he established. We need to be served by God and we need to be served by God's people. On Maundy Thursday, Jesus leads the way and we follow. Jesus' service is important because he shows us how to discern the true leaders from the false ones. He saw the false ones coming. He understood that wolves would come in to harass the sheep. Leaders who follow in the way of Christ lead with towel in hand. Jesus warns us, "You know that those who are regarded as rulers of the Gentiles lord it over them, and their high officials exercise authority over them. Not so with you. Instead, whoever wants to become great among you must be your servant" (Mark 10:42-43).

I'm not sure it's better to wash each other's feet once per month instead of annually. I am convinced we need to heed Jesus' reminder that love involves both giving and receiving service.

The central feature of the Maundy Thursday liturgy is a recounting of the Last Supper. On this night, Jesus took the rituals of the Jewish Passover and reinterpreted them in light of his impending death. He is the sacrifice who will bring about a new exodus to a new inheritance and kingdom. As N. T. Wright says, "When Jesus wanted fully to explain what his forthcoming death was all about, he didn't give them a theory. He didn't even give them a set of scriptural texts. He gave them a meal."[7] Jesus gave his people a way of bringing the nourishing reality of his death into the worshiping life of the community.

Maundy Thursday allows us to keep the central fact of the Christian faith always before us. Christ, our Passover, has been sacrificed for us.

After Communion a ritual known as the Stripping of the Altar takes place. In many churches it is common to find flowers, candles, hangings, and a host of other decorations near the front of the church. The Stripping of the Altar involves removing all those things until only the cross remains. The church has found her center. When all is stripped away, the hope of the world is the cross.

There is no dismissal after the altar is cleared. We have entered holy time. Like the disciples, we exit the church in silence, fleeing into the darkness. It's a custom in some churches to hold a prayer vigil that lasts from Maundy

Thursday until Good Friday. Just as Jesus told his disciples to watch and pray with him on that Thursday evening, the church watches and prays. But we know that the first disciples failed in their vigil. They fell asleep, and when temptation came they fell away. Even if we complete the liturgical actions of the vigil, we know we too have failed to keep watch. Confronted with suffering alongside Jesus, we also fled into darkness. We refused the cross.

The good news is that Jesus did not. He was willing to drink the cup.

Good Friday

Good Friday is the most solemn day on the church calendar. The irony of the day is included in its title—it is a "good" Friday, the best of all Fridays. It is also a tragedy that sums up all the tragedies of the human experience. It contains all the stuff of our existence. The innocent suffer, the powerful dismiss the weak for politically expedient reasons, and those who have put their hope in God see their dreams dashed. Good Friday is filled to the brim with blood, injustice, and death.

The dress of the clergy in the Anglican tradition matches the somberness of the day. The clergy process into the church in silence without an opening hymn. Robed in black cassocks, the clergy travel down the center aisle and declare, "All we like sheep have gone astray; we have turned every one to his own way" (Isaiah 53:6 KJV).

The season of fasting and prayer has prepared us for this. It has given us space to see who we are and who Jesus is. We have looked within ourselves and outward on the world around us. We know the truth that compels every Christian to flee to the cross to find succor. We have all gone astray. In ways large and small we have rebelled against God. We are not innocent. We have sinned and fallen short of the glory of God (Romans 3:23). We were given this glorious gift of the human experience: minds to reason, hearts to love, bodies to serve God and humanity. But we have made a mess of things. We have wounded and hurt and lied and rebelled. We are subject to judgment.

God's answer to this state of affairs is found in the response the congregation gives to the priest's confession of our waywardness: "And the LORD has laid on him the iniquity of us all" (Isaiah 53:6).

I am not separate from the events that happen on this day. I am caught up in them, not merely as a believer participating in a liturgy, but as a transgressor whose sins alongside the misdeeds of so many others made the cross necessary.

In the prayer for this day, we ask God to see us, saying, "We beseech thee graciously to behold this thy family, for which our Lord Jesus Christ was contented to be betrayed, and given up into the hands of wicked men, and to suffer death upon the cross."[8] We ask God to turn his eye to the trouble we have gotten ourselves into, but we do not want justice. Instead, we long for God to look on his people with the graciousness he promised was indicative of his very nature (Exodus 34:6). The good news in this prayer stands as a central theme of Christianity writ large: God sees us through the lens of his Son's sacrifice. He always gazes on us with grace. The prayer, then, is not to remind God of his duties, but to remind us of the source of our hope.

The readings are similar to those we encountered on Palm Sunday. Psalm 22, Isaiah 52–53, and the passion narrative return. But now they are in the spotlight. We are asked to sit with the fullness of Jesus' suffering on our behalf.

The cross forces us to take seriously our sins and those of the world. Our trespasses are of grave concern. We turn to our left and our right and see the carnage caused by evils perpetrated by people. These sins are both societal and intimately personal. We know of men and women who turn their homes into places of abuse. We are aware of teachers whose harsh words wound the aspirations of the young. We observe sexism, racism, and xenophobia. We are familiar with the predators who seek out the vulnerable. Widening the lens even more, we see famine caused by greed. We witness wars that leave the landscape and communities in ruin. We look on all we have done, and we call it bad. The wages of sin is indeed death.

Paul's cry, "Who will rescue me from this body of death?" (Romans 7:24 NRSV), must be owned as the ache of every human heart. Yes, the problem is serious and seems overwhelming, but Good Friday is not the story of tragedy but of triumph.

In the Anglican tradition, we read John's account of the Passion of Christ, which includes Jesus' encounter with Pilate. After Pilate has ordered Jesus' flogging, he has Jesus appear before the multitude and says, "Behold the person!" (John 19:5 my translation). Pilate may have thought he was just showing Jesus to the crowd, but the Gospel writer sees more in that statement. Pilate was displaying Jesus to the world. Jesus, precisely as the completely innocent and faithful one, beaten and bloody, was the person. If humanity is defined by a life oriented to God, Jesus was the first truly human person to exist. We call deep evil "inhumane" because there is something about sin and evil that is out of accord with the purpose for which we were created. It is subhuman. We needed Jesus' consistent faithfulness to God to demonstrate the truly human life and blaze a path for us to follow.

Jesus is the beginning of the resistance. In him God declares that sin and death will not always rule. Jesus' fidelity to God in the face of evil is the wellspring of power that gives us the strength to live a fully human life. The cross of Christ is not an ending, a final act of evil in a world that knows only the destruction of good. The cross is evil meeting a more powerful foe: Emmanuel God with us, even unto death.

So we weep at the evil our sins have caused, but we also rejoice in the glory of God. We remember the price by which we were purchased and the life it opened up to us. We find our strength at the cross, where God's Son became weak for us.

There is only one day of the church year in which there is no celebration of the Eucharist: Good Friday. Some churches distribute bread and wine from reserves left over from Maundy Thursday, but there is no consecration of the elements. On this day we recall the sacrifice to which the Eucharist bears witness. It's not a large thing, but I do not receive the reserved elements on this day. It's fine on this day to fast even from the bread and wine, to give myself space to ponder the work of the cross.

I am a child of the Reformation, and I believe that its great emphases on the grace of God and the finished work of Christ are important. But I must confess that endless debates over theories of the atonement do not stir my imagination or devotion. Yes, there are false and poor ways of talking about the cross, but there is no escaping the fact I cannot comprehend that Jesus paid a price for our reconciliation.

Few works of scholarship capture my feelings about the cross better than the prayer that marks the end of Good Friday. It seems fitting, then, to conclude my discussion of this most sacred of days with a reflection on it.

> Lord Jesus Christ, Son of the Living God, we pray you to set your passion, cross, and death between your judgment and our souls, now and in the hour of our death. Give mercy and grace to the living;

pardon and rest to the dead; to your holy Church peace and concord; and to us sinners everlasting life and glory; for with the Father and the Holy Spirit you live and reign, one God, now and forever. Amen.[9]

This is my plea and the cry of every Christian. When the time for judgment comes and we must present our case, we do not bring before the throne of the living God a list of our accomplishments. We will not say, "Lord, I kept the fast, I avoided meat for forty days, I increased the fervency of my prayers, and I read the entire Bible cover to cover." We will not boast of our tithes or acts of service.

We will tell our Creator what he already knows: "You sent your Son Jesus to live among us as God made flesh. He was a prophet mighty in word and dead. He was the long-hoped-for king and our great high priest. But we did not recognize him as such. We rejected him. And he died on the cross for our sins. But you raised him up by your mighty power. He appeared to the women and then the remaining apostles. He sent them into the world to spread the good news of his defeat of death and his coming kingdom. This kingdom is accessible to all who put their trust in his saving work. Through the twists and turns of history the gospel made its way throughout the world, eventually coming to a Black Baptist church in Huntsville, Alabama. They told me about your Son, and I believed. I've made a mess of things a hundred times over, but I believed it then and I believe it still.

Christ died for me and called me to himself. He promised to save me at the last. Now that I come to the last, I plead the blood!

The details may be different for you. You may have heard the gospel in a different place, at a different time, or in a different way. But you, too, need something to come between God's righteous judgment and your soul. We know no other hope.

But this plea is not merely for the Last Judgment. It is our constant cry whenever sin crouches at our door. The Passion of Christ is God's final command to put sin in its place. It is a reminder that we belong to one who has overcome it. I trust that will be enough.

As on Maundy Thursday, the people depart from the Good Friday service in silence. We are still in the midst of holy time. There is more to see and do before this week is finished.

Holy Saturday: It Is Time to Rest

On Maundy Thursday we remember the inauguration of the Eucharist and Jesus' command to love one another. That love manifests itself in service, as seen in Jesus' washing of the disciples' feet. Good Friday is a much darker affair. The disciples have fled, and Jesus must complete the work his Father has given him to do. The third service of the Triduum is Easter Vigil. Most churches pick up here. This service tells the whole of God's redemptive story from beginning to end, climaxing with the acclamation that Christ is risen. But the story of Easter and its aftermath is for the next book in this series.

Sadly, many churches have lost sight of a little service nestled between Good Friday and the Vigil. It is a fitting conclusion to our discussion of Lent because its central theme is rest from our labors.

It is called Holy Saturday. This gem of a service reflects on the time between Jesus' death and resurrection.[10] The prayer for Holy Saturday reminds us Jesus' body was laid in the tomb and took its rest on the Sabbath.

> O God, Creator of heaven and earth: Grant that, as the crucified body of your dear Son was laid in the tomb and rested on this holy Sabbath, so we may

await with him the coming of the third day, and rise with him to newness of life; who now lives and reigns with you and the Holy Spirit, one God, for ever and ever. Amen.[11]

This prayer calls on us to wait with Jesus for the coming on the third day. It invites us to trust that, even amid the darkest trials, something good may yet emerge. If we consider for a moment the radical difference between Jesus' experience of Holy Saturday and that of the disciples, we begin to understand how awe inspiring the Holy Saturday prayer is and the supreme challenge it poses to us.

At this point in the Gospel story, there is no work left for the disciples to do. There are no more great deeds to perform. All that remains is the waiting. Holy Saturday reminds us—as the Sabbath itself does—that for all our activity, our hope is not in the things we accomplish. Many times I have wrestled in prayer over some dilemma and found there was no good solution, at least not one I could discern. All fruitful paths seemed closed and there was nothing to do but wait.

Eventually, we all come to this place of waiting. We run out of room for human action. God will act or we are lost.

This happens in relationships, careers, and even the human body. We can run and diet and get all the rest we want. Death still comes for us in the end.

The Scriptures from Holy Saturday resound with questions about death. The Old Testament reading, Job 14:1-14, wonders: "If someone dies, will they live again?" (v. 14). Psalm 88, also appointed on this morning, inquires,

> Do you show your wonders to the dead?
> Do their spirits rise up and praise you?
> Is your love declared in the grave,
> your faithfulness in Destruction? (Psalm 88:10-11)

The Christian may say that God's reply is yes, but the psalmist is pressing ultimate questions during a time of real pain and sorrow.

These readings and our constant striving reveal our anxieties about the limits of God's power. Why else are we so constantly afraid? In times of trauma, aren't we tempted to wonder if this particular problem is too big for God? God may have been sufficient when we were younger, but what can he do when our marriage is in trouble or the loneliness of another year stretches before us? What will God do about the darkness in our heart that we just can't shake? When will he do something about the pain we see all around?

The disciples must have considered these questions on Holy Saturday. They hid for a reason. They "had hoped that he was the one who was going to redeem Israel" (Luke 24:21), but now all appeared lost. The crucifixion of Jesus seemed to be a tragedy so all-encompassing there was no future. What good were all those things he had taught them if death still ruled over him? The experience of the disciples in the wake of Jesus' death stands in for all our disappointments. We too have moments when it appears as if God failed us. There are seemingly unanswered prayers that will trouble us until we see him face-to-face.

Jesus' death, then, was not a momentary tragedy. It threw the disciples' last three years with him into question. Had it all been a waste? This is the doubt that seeps into our prayers, too, when we are alone with our fears. Are we fools after all, trusting in the fantastic stories of a premodern world not yet come of age?

I have never understood those who consider Jesus merely a good teacher. His teachings revealed his divinity. He predicted his resurrection and his defeat of death. If he was wrong on this most central of questions (his own divine identity), he is of no use to us. Let us weep, because only darkness awaits us.

The good news of Holy Saturday is not that the disciples waited with faith. They did not. Often, we do not either. There are moments when the traumas in our lives are too much and we are overcome with despair. Sometimes it is all just too much for us.

But God does not share our anxieties. The latest theory claiming to disprove his existence does not trouble him nor do supposed threats to his power. As the psalm reminds us, "He who sits in the heavens laughs; the LORD has them in derision" (Psalm 2:4 NRSV). Christ knew he would rise again. If the experience of the disciples stands in for our fears, then the peace of Christ serves as God's answer to our troubled hearts. We can be at peace because God reigns even over the death that unnerves us. We end Lent with the confidence that all will be well.

This is how the season of Lent concludes. Things are quiet. We are silent. We stand at the tomb wondering what God will do next. Whether we have kept our fasts or failed has no bearing on the final outcome. God either has the power to raise Christ from the dead, or he does not. We are Christians because we have concluded that he does. That means we can rest.

Conclusion

Some who are reading this will be on the verge of baptism. I pray this book and the season it describes prepare you for the joyous life with God that awaits. Other readers will have walked with Jesus many years. I pray that this Lent and all those that follow remind you of the sweetness of our salvation and the joy that comes with following Jesus. All these rituals, prayers, and ceremonies are simply doorways into the thing itself: God in all his splendor. May we find him afresh every year until we see him face-to-face.

In Lent we learn that God does more than make up for our inadequacies. He does not finish a race we began or fill what is lacking in our sacrifices. The whole thing is his own work all along. He renders our efforts irrelevant to the question of our life with him. He makes it all a matter of grace.

Our prayers, good deeds, fasts, and Scripture readings earn us nothing. Instead, they are Spirit-empowered means of entering into communion with Christ. They are about sharing the thing itself—the divine life. It's a gift we too easily cast aside. Lent reminds us that the opportunity to reclaim that gift is always near—as near as the resurrection itself.

Acknowledgments

I would like to thank Michael Morse, the first clergy-person who helped me appreciate how God can form us through the great tradition. I am a better clergyperson and Christian for having known you. I also want to express my gratitude to Nashotah House for teaching me the depths of the tradition that has been so life giving to me.

I would also like to thank Ethan McCarthy, Anna Gissing, and the people of IVP for their support and belief in this project. I would also like to express my gratitude to all the writers in this series for offering their gifts to the church and the world through writing.

Finally, to my children, Miriam, Peter, Clare, and Luke, I hope that the great tradition of Christian faith and practice brings as much joy to you as it has to me.

Notes

We Must Repent

[1]Martin Luther, "The 95 Theses," 500 Jahre Reformation, accessed April 8, 2022, www.luther.de/en/95thesen.html.

[2]Maxwell E. Johnson, "Lent," *Westminster Dictionary of Liturgy and Worship*, ed. Paul Bradshaw (Louisville, KY: Westminster John Knox, 2002), 278-79.

[3]Paul F. Bradshaw and Maxwell E. Johnson, *The Origins of Feasts, Fasts, and Seasons in Early Christianity* (Collegeville, MN: Liturgical Press, 2011), 98.

[4]To get to thirty-six days, you had five days per week for seven weeks and then Holy Saturday, which was a fast day.

[5]"Lent," *The Oxford Dictionary of the Christian Church*, eds. F. L. Cross and A. Livingstone (Oxford, UK: Oxford University Press, 2005), 971.

1. Facing Death, Finding Hope

[1]1662 Book of Common Prayer: International Edition, 122.

[2]1662 Book of Common Prayer: International Edition, 122.

[3]Book of Common Prayer, 1979, 268.

[4]Book of Common Prayer, 1979, 268.

[5]Book of Common Prayer, 1979, 268.

2. WHAT DO THESE THINGS MEAN?

[1]Quoted in L. W. Cowie and John Selwyn Gummer, *The Christian Calendar: A Complete Guide to the Seasons of the Christian Year* (Springfield, MA: G & C Merriam, 1974), 52.

[2]1662 Book of Common Prayer: International Edition, 252.

[3]1662 Book of Common Prayer: International Edition, 253.

[4]1662 Book of Common Prayer: International Edition, 253.

[5]The Book of Occasional Services, 2003, 59.

[6]Robert E. Webber, *Ancient Future Time: Forming Spirituality Through the Christian Year* (Grand Rapids, MI: Baker Books, 2004), 131.

[7]Taken from The Book of Occasional Services, 2003, 59-73.

[8]The Book of Occasional Services, 2003, 71.

3. WHAT WE HAVE RECEIVED

[1]Book of Common Prayer, 1979, 166. There are a variety of collects and arrangement of these prayers of Lent. I have chosen to follow the 1979 Book of Common Prayer, the one I used during my first Lent and the one with which I have had the longest opportunity to reflect.

[2]Book of Common Prayer, 1979, 166-67.

[3]Book of Common Prayer, 1979, 218.

[4]Robert Lowry and Annie S. Hawks, "I Need Thee Every Hour," Hymnary.org, 1872, hymnary.org/text/i_need_thee_every_hour_most_gracious_lor.

[5]Book of Common Prayer, 1979, 219.

[6]Book of Common Prayer, 1979, 219.

4. HE LOVED US TO THE END

[1]St. Theodulph of Orleans, "All Glory, Laud, and Honor," trans. J. M. Neale, Hymnary.org, c. 820, hymnary.org/text/all_glory_laud_and_honor.

[2]Book of Common Prayer, 1979, 271.

[3]Henry Hart Milman, "Ride On! Ride On in Majesty!," Hymnary.org, 1827, hymnary.org/text/ride_on_ride_on_in_majesty.

[4]Adapted from Esau McCaulley, "The Palms, the Temple, and the Nations," *Christianity Today,* March 23, 2018, www.christianitytoday .com/ct/2018/march-web-only/palms-temple-nations-palm-sunday -reconciliation.html.

[5]Book of Common Prayer, 1979, 274.

[6]This section is lightly adapted from my previous writings on the subject, which can be found here: "Give Me Your Feet and I Will Give You Mine: Footwashing Amongst the Baptists and Episcopalians," Esau McCaulley (blog), March 24, 2016, http://esaumccaulley.com /give-me-your-feet-and-i-will-give-you-mine-footwashing-amongst -the-baptists-and-episcopalians/.

[7]N. T. Wright, *Simply Jesus: A New Vision of Who He Was, What He Did, and Why He Matters* (New York: Harper One, 2011), 179.

[8]1662 Book of Common Prayer: International Edition, 127.

[9]Book of Common Prayer, 1979, 282.

[10]Adapted from my previous reflections: "Holy Saturday: The Earth Holds Its Breath," Esau McCaulley (blog), April 11, 2020, http:// esaumccaulley.com/holy-saturday-the-earth-holds-its-breath/.

[11]Book of Common Prayer, 1979, 283.

The Fullness of Time Series

Each volume in the Fullness of Time series invites readers to engage with the riches of the church year, exploring the traditions, prayers, Scriptures, and rituals of the seasons of the church calendar.

LENT

Esau McCaulley

ADVENT

Tish Harrison Warren

EASTER

Wesley Hill

CHRISTMAS

Emily McGowin

PENTECOST

Emilio Alvarez

EPIPHANY

Fleming Rutledge